PLAY BALL!

Baseball Tips and Tricks

RACHEL STUCKEY

CRABTREE
Publishing Company
www.crabtreebooks.com

Author
Rachel Stuckey

Editors
Marcia Abramson, Kelly Spence

Photo research
Melissa McClellan

Design
T. J. Choleva

Cover Design
Samara Parent

Prepress Technician
Samara Parent

Production coordinator
Margaret Amy Salter

Produced for Crabtree Publishing by
BlueAppleWorks Inc.

Consultant
James L. Gates Jr., Library Director
National Baseball Hall of Fame and Museum

Photographs
Front Cover: Thinkstock
Interior
Bigstock: © karenfoleyphotography (p 6–7 top); © neilld (p 24); © Ffooter
(p 27 bottom)
Creative Commons: LiAnna Davis (p 5 left); Gary Soup (p 13 bottom); Keith
Allison (p 21 bottom)
Keystone Press: © Scott Serio (p 14 left, 19 bottom); © Kenneth K. Lam (p 15 left);
© Michael S. Wirtz (p 17 bottom); © Peter Joneleit/Cal Sport Media (p 27 right);
© Stephen Wise (p 13 top, 17 top, 21 top)
Shutterstock.com: © tammykayphoto (title page); © Mike Flippo (TOC top);
© James R. Martin (TOC background); © Ben Carlson (chapter page topper);
© David Lee (page toppers); © Africa Studio (baseball); © Natchapon (p 4);
© Paul McKinnon (p 4 right);
© Ffooter (p 6 bottom); Eric Broder Van Dyke (p 7 bottom, 12 bottom, 22–23
bottom); © KPG_Payless (p 7 top); © tammykayphoto (p 7 bottom right, 15
top); © Shawn Pecor (p 10 top, 12 right); © Photo Works (p 11 bottom); © Steve
Broer (p 12–13 top, 18–19 top); © Jamie Roach (p 13 middle, 25 right); © Nicolesa
(p 15 bottom); © Peter Weber (p 16); © Arthur Eugene Preston (p 18 left);
© Eugene Buchko (18–19 bottom); © Aspen Photo (p 19 top, 20, 22 left, 29 right);
© gary yim (p 22–23 top); © Bill Florence (p 23 left); © bikeriderlondon (p 23
right); © Rena Schild (p 25 left); © Alan C. Heison (p 28)
Thinkstock: Ingram Publishing (p 5 top); © Fuse (p 8, 26, 30); Jupiterimages
(p 10, 14 right, 29 top); © James Peragine (p 11 middle); © Comstock (p 12 left)

Library and Archives Canada Cataloguing in Publication

Stuckey, Rachel, author
    Play ball! : baseball tips and tricks / Rachel Stuckey.

(Baseball source)
Includes index.
Issued in print and electronic formats.
ISBN 978-0-7787-1478-1 (bound).--ISBN 978-0-7787-1871-0 (pbk.).--
ISBN 978-1-4271-7619-6 (pdf).--ISBN 978-1-4271-7615-8 (html)

    1. Baseball--Juvenile literature. I. Title. II. Title: Baseball tips
and tricks.

GV867.5.S78 2015   j796.357   C2014-908295-9
                                             C2014-908296-7

Library of Congress Cataloging-in-Publication Data

CIP available at the Library of Congress

Crabtree Publishing Company

www.crabtreebooks.com   1-800-387-7650

Printed in Canada/042015/BF20150203

Published in Canada
Crabtree Publishing
616 Welland Ave.
St. Catharines, ON
L2M 5V6

Published in the United States
Crabtree Publishing
PMB 59051
350 Fifth Avenue, 59th Floor
New York, New York 10118

Published in the United Kingdom
Crabtree Publishing
Maritime House
Basin Road North, Hove
BN41 1WR

Published in Australia
Crabtree Publishing
3 Charles Street
Coburg North
VIC 3058

CONTENTS

Baseball Around the World   4

How to Play   6

Warming Up   8

Batter Up!   10

Running the Bases   12

Fielding the Ball   14

Throwing the Ball   16

Get into the Game   18

On Top of the Mound   20

Catch Me If You Can   22

Inside the Diamond   24

In the Outfield   26

Sportsmanship   28

Play like a Pro   30

Learning More   31

Glossary and Index   32

LET'S PLAY BALL!

BASEBALL AROUND THE WORLD

The modern game of baseball was born in the 1840s in the northeastern United States. Before long, it became very popular! Baseball may be known as "America's Pastime," but the game is loved all over the world in countries such as Canada, Mexico, the Dominican Republic, Cuba, Venezuela, Japan, South Korea, Taiwan, and Australia.

Baseball Leagues in North America

Both men and women play baseball at many different levels. In professional baseball, players are paid money to play. Major League Baseball (MLB) includes the American League and the National League, with teams across the United States and Canada. Minor League Baseball is also a professional league made up of smaller, local leagues all over North America.

Nearly 74 million spectators attended MLB games in 2014. No other pro sports league draws as many fans.

Fun for All Ages

Children and teenagers can play baseball on school teams and in youth leagues. Teams from all over the world compete in the Little League® World Series every year. Colleges and universities also have baseball teams.

Around the World

Enthusiastic baseball fans are found everywhere. Professional leagues were founded in many Latin American countries, Asia, and Europe. Every four years, the best players from 16 countries step up to the plate to compete in the World Baseball Classic. This international tournament promotes and celebrates the game around the world.

Professional players compete for their countries in the World Baseball Classic. The next one is planned for 2017.

Softball

Softball was invented in Chicago in the 1880s. It started as an indoor game similar to baseball, which is why a softball field is smaller than a baseball diamond. The balls are larger than baseballs, but not actually softer. The ball is pitched underhand in a style called the windmill. Because women play softball at the college and international level, many people think of softball as "girls' baseball." But both men and women play. Softball is the most popular **recreational** sport in North America. There are many kinds of softball with slower pitching that make it easier to hit the ball.

5

HOW TO PLAY

Baseball is played on a diamond with a bat and a ball. Home plate and the three bases form the shape of a diamond. The pitcher stands on a **mound**, or small hill, in the middle of the diamond. In professional baseball, the distance between each base is 90 feet (27 m), and the pitcher's mound is 60 feet and 6 inches (18.5 m) from home plate. Lines run from home plate to first and third bases and then continue into the field. These lines are the boundaries of play.

Players and umpires have assigned positions during a game.

5

Outfield (Grass)

5

5

6

4

4

4

6

4

Second Base

Infield (Dirt)

4

6

1

Pitcher's Mound

Third Base

Infield (Grass)

First Base

Home Plate

2

6

3

1. Pitcher	4. Infielders
2. Batter	5. Outfielders
3. Catcher	6. Umpires

Playing the Ball

In a game, the pitcher throws the ball to home plate and the batter tries to hit the ball. Good pitches are called **strikes**. Pitches outside the **strike zone** are **balls**. If a batter swings and misses, that is also a strike. A batter with three strikes is **out**. After four balls, the batter gets **walked** to first base.

After hitting the ball, a player must run safely to each of the three bases and then back to home plate to score a **run**. When the ball is hit, the batter runs to first base.

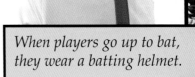

When players go up to bat, they wear a batting helmet.

If a fielder catches the ball in the air, the runner is out. If the ball hits the ground, fielders must throw it to the base before the runner, or **tag**, or touch, him or her with the ball. If they do not, the runner is **safe**. If a ball is hit outside the lines of play, a **foul** is called and the batter gets to hit again. After three outs, the teams switch. Baseball games have nine **innings**, or periods. Each inning, both teams get a chance to bat and field.

Baseball players wear long pants, a shirt, and a hat. They also wear shoes with spikes to help them run without slipping. When playing in the field, players use a glove to catch the ball.

WARMING UP

Baseball can seem like a slow game, but players must be ready to react and move quickly when each play begins. Always warm up before practices and games to avoid getting hurt. Doing static stretches on cold muscles can cause injury, so start with a few minutes of jogging. Then, do some **dynamic**, or active, stretching, such as walking lunges, side steps, and leg swings. Baseball players use their whole bodies, so it's important to also warm up your arms and upper body. Arm circles, shoulder circles, and side bends are good upper-body stretches to try.

Warming up and stretching as a team helps make sure everyone is ready to go when the game begins.

Watch the Ball!

After warming up their bodies, baseball players must also warm up their skills. Start by throwing the ball back and forth with a teammate to loosen up your arm. Your coach may throw or hit balls into the field so players can practice fielding the ball and making plays. There may be lots of balls flying through the air during a warm-up, so pay attention. Keep your eyes open!

Baseball players practice both individually and as a team to improve their skills. There are special drills for pitching, catching, hitting, fielding, throwing, and running the bases.

Get Moving!

Leg Swings—Hold on to a fence and stand tall on one foot. Swing the other leg from front to back. Repeat! Then, turn to face the fence and hold on for balance. Lift your leg out to the side. Swing your leg in front of your other leg and back out to the side. Repeat!

Walking Lunges—Step forward with one leg and bend at the knee. Then, lift your back leg up to walk forward and bend at the knee again. Repeat!

Shoulder Circles—Lift your shoulders up and roll them forward, down, and back in a circle. Then, do the same movement in the other direction.

Arm Swings—Hold your arms straight out at your sides. Make small circles with your arms, then make them bigger. Switch directions.

BATTER UP!

Hitting a baseball is one of the hardest things to do in sports. Batters must keep their eyes on the ball and then swing the bat at just the right moment. To start, stand facing home plate with most of your weight on your back foot and your knees slightly bent. Hold the bat with both hands together, your elbows up, with the bat in the air over your back shoulder. This is called the **batting stance**. Look over your front shoulder to watch the pitcher. When you swing, straighten your arms and pull them all the way around while also shifting your weight to your front leg. The swing should be one smooth motion.

OFF THE BAT!

Players can wear batting gloves on one or both hands to get a better grip on the bat. Gloves also prevent blisters and absorb some of the vibrations that travel down the bat when it hits the ball.

The three basic batting stances are open, closed, and even, depending on the position of the batter's feet. Batters should choose stances that feel relaxed and comfortable.

Batters need quick reflexes because some pitches, such as a good fastball, can travel from the mound to home plate in a fraction of a second.

Batting Drill

Teeball is a baseball game for little kids. The ball sits on a tall rubber tee at home plate. Because the ball isn't moving, you can focus on your stance, your swing, keeping your eye on the ball, and connecting with the ball. For practice, try using a tennis ball or even a **Wiffle** ball.

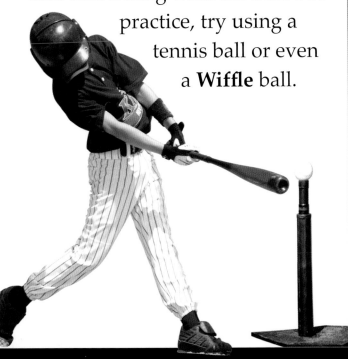

Miguel Cabrera

Miguel Cabrera is one of the best hitters in baseball. In 2012 he won the Triple Crown of batting, with the best **batting average** (.330), the most home runs (44), and the most **RBIs** (139) that year. He has played for the Florida Marlins and the Detroit Tigers.

NESN

Once you make it to first base, you are a **base runner**. If you are on first base when the ball is hit, you must run to second base. If the second baseman receives the ball before you get there, you are out. This is called a **force out**. If you are on second or third base, and there is no runner behind you, the baseman must touch you with the ball. This is called a **tag out**. Base runners sometimes slide into the base to avoid the tag. It's more difficult for a baseman to make a tag if the runner is down low.

An umpire calls a base runner safe at home. This means the catcher did not tag the runner with the ball before he or she reached home plate.

Stealing a Base

Base runners also steal bases when there is no hit. Base runners take a **lead off** base, then take off running when the pitch begins. The runner must get to the next base before the catcher or pitcher throws the ball to the baseman—or else he or she is out!

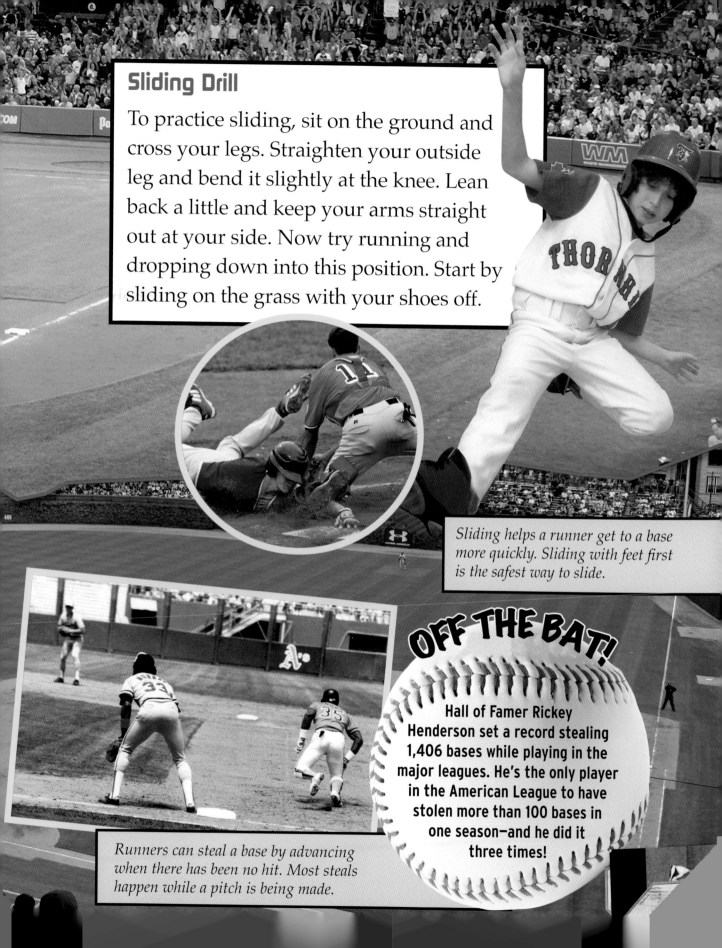

Sliding Drill

To practice sliding, sit on the ground and cross your legs. Straighten your outside leg and bend it slightly at the knee. Lean back a little and keep your arms straight out at your side. Now try running and dropping down into this position. Start by sliding on the grass with your shoes off.

Sliding helps a runner get to a base more quickly. Sliding with feet first is the safest way to slide.

OFF THE BAT!

Hall of Famer Rickey Henderson set a record stealing 1,406 bases while playing in the major leagues. He's the only player in the American League to have stolen more than 100 bases in one season—and he did it three times!

Runners can steal a base by advancing when there has been no hit. Most steals happen while a pitch is being made.

FIELDING THE BALL

Players use gloves to field the ball after the batter hits a pitch. There are five basic hits. A **fly ball** is hit into the air. A **pop-up** is a fly ball that is hit very high but does not travel very far. A **line drive** goes through the air but not very high. If these hits are caught before hitting the ground, the batter is out. A ground ball, or **grounder**, rolls or bounces across the field. A **bunt** is when the batter uses the bat to block the ball instead of swinging—the ball does not travel very far. A fast runner can sometimes beat the throw to first base.

When a hit ball rolls or bounces before being fielded, it is called a grounder. If the runner reaches base safely, it is a hit. If not, it is a ground out.

When a fielder catches a hit ball in the air, the batter is automatically out.

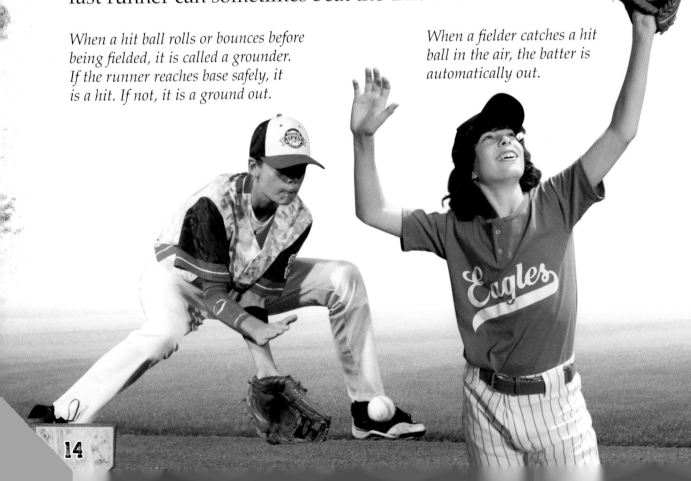

Catching Drill

When learning to catch a ball, start with your bare hands and a tennis or Wiffle ball. Then practice catching a baseball with your bare hands. Once you've mastered that, you can start working with your glove. Use your throwing hand to help trap and cradle the ball in your glove.

Adam Jones won the Gold Glove in 2009, 2012, 2013, and 2014 playing center field for the Baltimore Orioles.

OFF THE BAT!

Each year, the managers and coaches in Major League Baseball vote for the players who did the best job of fielding. These players win a Gold Glove Award.

What's in a Glove?

Baseball gloves have webbing between the thumb and fingers to help catch the ball. There are different types of baseball gloves for each position. Infielders use small, light gloves so they can get the ball out of their gloves quickly to make plays. Outfielders use long gloves to help them reach for fly balls. Catchers' gloves are called **mitts** and have lots of padding. First basemen's gloves are extra large and, like catchers', are also called mitts.

THROWING THE BALL

When you throw a baseball, you use your entire body. To start, grip the ball with two fingers and your thumb. Hold the ball in your glove in front of your chest. Stand with your feet apart, with your glove arm facing your target. Keep your glove-side elbow pointed at your target. Circle your throwing arm down and around. Take a small step with your front leg and turn your upper body toward your target. Release the ball with a bend of your wrist.

Along with mastering different pitches, a pitcher must stay focused. The mental game is just as important as throwing properly.

Target Practice

If you don't have anyone to catch your throws, you can use a brick or cement wall to practice your **accuracy**. Set up a target and practice hitting the target with a tennis ball. Take a few steps back to practice throwing from farther away.

A pitcher aims to throw strikes and not give up base hits or walks. Practicing with a target helps a pitcher keep the ball in the strike zone.

Mo'ne was named Sports Illustrated's Sports Kid of the Year in 2014.

OFF THE BAT!

The phrase "you throw like a girl" comes from the days when little girls didn't learn how to throw a ball. But 13-year-old Mo'ne Davis has changed the meaning of that phrase! Mo'ne throws a fastball at 70 miles per hour (113 kmph). She also pitched a no-hitter in the 2014 Little League® World Series.

What's in a Ball?

Baseballs are about nine inches (23 cm) around. They are covered in two pieces of white leather connected with red stitches. Underneath the leather, a rubber or cork core is wrapped in yarn. The stiches help players grip the ball.

GET INTO THE GAME

During most games, every player on the field also gets a turn at bat. That means everyone plays both **offense** and **defense**. However, some leagues allow for **designated hitters**. These are batters that do not play in the field, and pitchers for these teams do not hit. Each team has nine players on the field or in the batting lineup. Extra players on the team can replace players on the field or at bat. In professional baseball, once you've left the game, you can't come back.

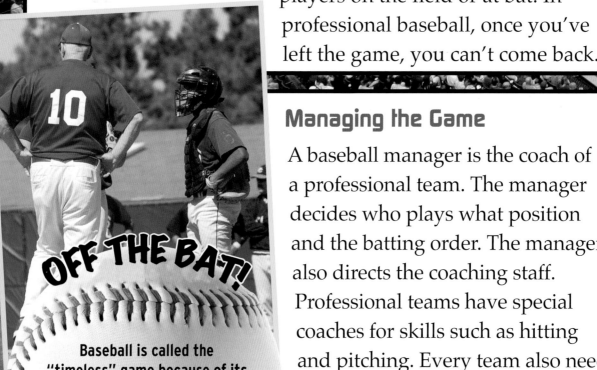

OFF THE BAT!

Baseball is called the "timeless" game because of its long history. But it is also one of the only sports that has no official time keeping. There are no time limits in baseball.

Managing the Game

A baseball manager is the coach of a professional team. The manager decides who plays what position and the batting order. The manager also directs the coaching staff. Professional teams have special coaches for skills such as hitting and pitching. Every team also needs a first base coach and a third base coach. Base coaches tell runners if they should stop or keep going, so that players focus on running and not what's happening on the field.

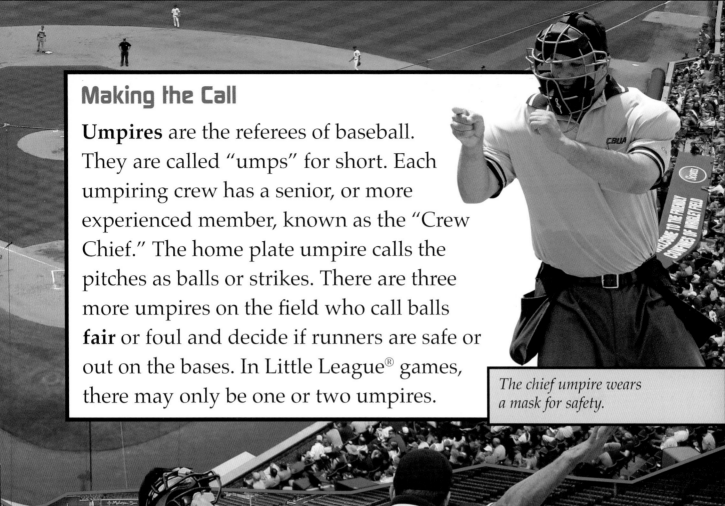

Making the Call

Umpires are the referees of baseball. They are called "umps" for short. Each umpiring crew has a senior, or more experienced member, known as the "Crew Chief." The home plate umpire calls the pitches as balls or strikes. There are three more umpires on the field who call balls **fair** or foul and decide if runners are safe or out on the bases. In Little League® games, there may only be one or two umpires.

The chief umpire wears a mask for safety.

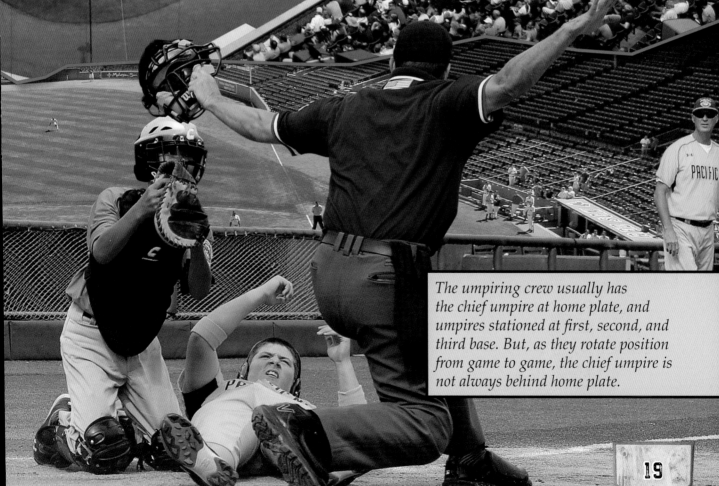

The umpiring crew usually has the chief umpire at home plate, and umpires stationed at first, second, and third base. But, as they rotate position from game to game, the chief umpire is not always behind home plate.

ON TOP OF THE MOUND

Each play begins when the pitcher throws the ball to the catcher at home plate. The goal of every pitcher is to get batters out, and to win the game. Pitchers often attempt to strike out the batters. But a good pitcher also throws pitches that make batters hit grounders and fly balls. These are the easiest hits for players to field. Good defense begins with the pitcher.

Fast-Throwing Pitchers

Pitchers throw different pitches depending on how they grip or hold the ball. Pitchers use the stitches of the baseball for different grips. Pitchers prepare for the pitch with the wind-up. With his or her back foot on the rubber, a pitcher lifts their front leg and pulls their upper body back. As he or she steps forward with their front leg, the pitcher uses their upper body to add power to the throw.

*Pitches come in two speeds, slow and fast, but there are many variations such as **change-ups**, **sliders**, and **sinkers**. Superstar MLB pitchers often have four pitches.*

Throwing from the Knee

Pitchers must have excellent control when they throw the ball. Try this knee throwing drill to focus on your throwing technique before learning the wind-up motion. Get down on one knee (on your throwing side). When you throw the ball, turn your upper body so your shoulder faces your target and your throwing arm is behind you. Rotate your body as you throw.

Aroldis Chapman

Aroldis Chapman is one of the fastest pitchers in MLB. In 2010, playing for the Cincinnati Reds, he threw a 105.1 mph (169 kmph) fastball. That's almost twice as fast as a car drives on a highway.

Albertin Aroldis Chapman de la Cruz is called the Cuban Missile because he throws so fast and is from Cuba.

CATCH ME IF YOU CAN

The team's catcher is considered a captain on the field. He or she is often in charge of planning defensive plays. The role of the catcher in baseball is demanding. A skilled catcher must have fast judgment as well as great leadership skills.

Catcher in Charge

Out of all players, only the catcher is positioned to see the entire field of play. He or she squats behind the plate in protective gear and controls every action. The catcher makes calls based on many important details that they process in a split second. The catcher must be aware of every aspect of the game at all times. He or she needs to know the strengths and weaknesses of the hitter (the opponent) and their own teammates. The catcher also must keep the score, the inning, and the number of outs in mind.

Catchers use a special mitt to catch balls. They also wear a mask, helmet, and padding to protect them from being hit by a wild pitch or foul ball.

Calling the Game

When a catcher makes a decision about the type of pitch to be delivered to home plate, he or she is said to be "**calling the game**." The catcher gives signs to the pitcher for what pitch to throw. Most of the time it is done through a number system. The catcher uses their fingers to signal the numbers to the pitcher. Each number represents a different pitch. The pitcher can either agree or disagree with a shake of their head. Some catchers give signals by touching certain parts of their chest protectors to confuse the oponents, especially when a runner happens to be on second base and can see the hand signals.

Catchers use their fingers to signal to the pitchers what kind of pitch to throw.

Catchers have to be fearless, as some pitchers throw the baseball as fast as 100 mph (161 kmph).

OFF THE BAT!

Yogi Berra of the New York Yankees was one of the greatest catchers in baseball history. He is also funny and well-known for his witty quotes called "Yogiisms," such as "It ain't over 'til it's over."

23

INSIDE THE DIAMOND

Many balls are hit to the infield, so a baseball team depends on good defense by its infielders. Infielders defend around the diamond area of the baseball field. Each team has a first baseman, second baseman, third baseman, and shortstop. The shortstop plays in between second and third bases. The second baseman and the shortstop cover the middle of the field, and the first baseman and third baseman cover the **baselines**. Infielders must catch the ball after it is hit or field it and throw to a base to make an out. When the second baseman fields the ball, the shortstop covers second base.

Infielders must be fast, smart, and agile. They have to make quick decisions about how to play a hit ball and where to throw it.

Passing the Ball

Infielders usually field grounders and throw the ball to first base for a force out. But if there is already a runner on first base, the infielders have the chance to get two force outs, better known as a **double play**. After stopping the ball, the player throws it to second base before the runner gets there. Then, the player on second base throws the ball to first base before the batter gets there.

*It is important for infielders to field the ball accurately and avoid making mistakes, which are called **errors** in baseball.*

Playing the Numbers

Each position on a baseball field has a number —the pitcher is 1, the catcher is 2, first base is 3, second base is 4, third base is 5, shortstop is 6, and the outfield is 7-8-9. Each play is recorded using these numbers. For example, 6-4-3 and 4-6-3 are the most common types of double plays.

Derek Jeter

Derek Jeter was the shortstop for the New York Yankees for 20 years. He won five Gold Gloves and five Silver Slugger awards. When Jeter retired in 2014, he had the most hits by a shortstop in major league history.

25

IN THE OUTFIELD

There are three outfielders on the field. Outfielders must catch or stop the balls that get past the infield. Outfielders usually catch fly balls to make outs. Sometimes a grounder will go all the way to the outfield, or a line drive will touch the ground before an outfielder can reach it. The outfielder must throw the ball into the infield as fast as he or she can to stop the batter from running around the bases. Instead of throwing the ball to a player at a base, outfielders are supposed to throw to the **cut-off**, an infielder who runs out to catch the throw. Using a cut-off is usually faster and more accurate.

Outfielders need speed to get to the ball, plus a strong arm for throwing it back to the infielders.

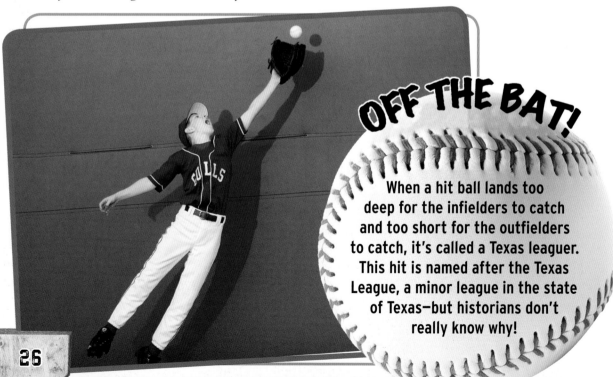

OFF THE BAT!

When a hit ball lands too deep for the infielders to catch and too short for the outfielders to catch, it's called a Texas leaguer. This hit is named after the Texas League, a minor league in the state of Texas—but historians don't really know why!

26

Chasing and Catching Balls

There are three positions in the outfield: left field, center field, and right field. The center fielder is usually the fastest of the three because he or she must cover the most ground. Left fielders field the ball more than right fielders, but right fielders usually have the strongest arms.

The outfield extends from the far edge of the infield dirt to the walls at the back of the baseball field. It divides into three sections: left, right, and center.

Mike Trout

Mike Trout won the American League Rookie of the Year award in 2012 while playing center field for the Anaheim Angels. In 2014 he was named the AL Most Valuable Player. Mike also won the Hank Aaron Award as the best hitter in the league.

Left Outfielder   *Center Outfielder*   *Right Outfielder*

SPORTSMANSHIP

Good baseball sportsmanship includes playing fair, following the rules, and respecting the umpires' decisions. If you are disrespectful toward the umpire, he or she can throw you out of the game. There are lots of official rules in baseball, but there are also some unwritten rules. Teammates can congratulate each other after scoring runs and making outs, but they can't show off.

High five! Good sportsmanship means celebrating a good play or win while still respecting the efforts of the other team and players.

For the Love of the Game

Players do not taunt their opponents when they strike out or miss the ball. Every experienced player knows that in baseball, you are just as likely to lose as you are to win. The best hitters in professional baseball only connect with the ball three out of every ten times. And on average, the best MLB teams only win five or six games out of every ten. To be a good ball player, you need to love playing the game more than just wanting to win.

At every level of play, organized baseball encourages good sportsmanship. Umpires can throw out players who behave badly.

Nutrition

Baseball may not be as fast and intense as sports such as hockey and basketball, but it still takes energy. Baseball players spend a lot of time being ready to move, and then they have to act quickly. Eating well and avoiding junk food will help keep your energy level up for both practice and game day. And because you play and practice baseball outside in the sun, it's important to stay hydrated. Drink plenty of water or other healthy drinks before, during, and after the game.

Baseball is a warm-weather game, so players must make sure to stay hydrated. It is also a good idea to wear sunscreen to protect yourself from sunburn.

29

PLAY LIKE A PRO

There are many different age and competition levels in baseball. Local youth leagues are for everyone who wants to play, and little kids often start by playing teeball. You can try out for competitive Little League® teams for kids 13 and under. The best Little League® teams compete in the Little League® World Series each year. Teenagers can also play in local leagues or for their school teams. The best high school players may be recruited to play on college teams or even in the minor leagues after they graduate.

Just for Fun

Schoolyard versions of baseball like kickball or stickball allow you to work on your throwing, catching, and hitting skills, even if you can't play a full game of baseball. Many adults play baseball and softball just for fun. Everybody can take a turn!

You can learn a lot from high school and college, or even the competitive youth leagues in your area.

LEARNING MORE

Check out these books and websites to find out more about how to play ball like a pro!

Books

Baseball by James Buckley Jr., DK Eyewitness Books, 2010

Play Baseball Like a Pro: Key Skills and Tips by Hans Hetrick, Capstone Press, 2011

Websites

Little League International
The official site of Little League® Baseball and Softball
www.littleleague.org

Baseball USA
The official site of USA Baseball
web.usabaseball.com

Baseball Canada
The official site of Baseball Canada
www.baseball.ca

GLOSSARY

Note: Some boldfaced words are defined where they appear in the book.

accuracy Being careful and precise

baselines The unseen lines between two bases

batting average A statistic determined by dividing the number of hits by the number of at-bats

bunt A hit that uses the bat to block the pitch; the ball does not travel very far

change-up A pitch thrown to look like a fastball but at a slower speed

cut-off The player who runs out to catch the throw from the outfield after a big hit

defense A team trying to prevent another from scoring

double play A defensive play when two outs are made

dynamic Always moving

fair A ball that lands within the foul lines or leaves the park within the foul lines

fly ball A ball that is hit high in the air and usually travels to the outfield

force out A play in which the runner is forced to advance and as a result is out

foul A hit ball that goes out of bounds

grounder A ball hit on the ground

lead off When a base runner takes a few steps away from the base before the pitch

line drive A hit that travels straight through the air before it lands on the ground but doesn't go very high

mitt A special gove worn by the catcher

offense A team trying to score on another

pop-up A fly ball that is hit very high in the air in the infield

RBIs Runs batted in by the hitter

recreational Played for fun

safe When a batter or base runner makes it to a base before the ball or without being tagged out

sinker A pitch that suddenly drops as it passes home plate

slider A fast pitch that curves toward home plate

strike A pitch that is inside the strike zone or a pitch that a batter swings on and misses

strike zone The area in front of a batter that pitches must be in to be called a strike by an umpire

tag out Any out made when the infielders touch the runner with the ball before the runner makes it safely to a base

walk When a pitcher throws four pitches outside the strike zone and the batter gets to walk to first base, also called a base-on-balls

Wiffle A hollow, plastic ball

INDEX

American League 4, 13, 27
America's Pastime 4
baseball field 25, 27
batting average 11
Cabrera, Miguel 11
Chapman, Aroldis 21
Davis, Mo'ne 17
double play 25

Drill 11, 13, 15, 21
Gold Glove 15, 25
Hank Aaron Award 27
Henderson, Rickey 13
Jones, Adam 15
Little League® World Series 5, 17, 30
Major League Baseball (MLB) 4, 15, 20, 21, 29
manager 15, 18

Minor League Baseball 4
Most Valuable Player 27
National League 4
Rookie of the Year 27
Silver Slugger 25
softball 5, 30
Texas leaguer 26
Triple Crown 11
Trout, Mike 27
umpire 6, 12, 19, 28